HEAL DEPRESSION HOLISTICALLY

Ashish Lal

ACKNOWLEDGEMENTS

In the creation of this book, "Heal Depression Holistically," I've been blessed with guidance and support from sources both seen and unseen.

I begin by expressing gratitude to the divine force that orchestrated specific people and circumstances, leading me through a challenging three-year period of depression. These trials became the catalyst for this holistic healing journey. If the lowest phase had not hit me, I would have never evolved so much. I came out of that phase so transformed from within that since then, no people or circumstance could ever touch my inner peace. My life has been nothing but beautiful after that.

To my father, whose unwavering commitment to daily Yoga and holistic exercises spanning over three decades inspired resilience and discipline in me. Your steadfast example illuminated the path toward healing without the need for medication.

My heartfelt appreciation extends to my mother for her unwavering emotional support during the darkest moments and beyond, illuminating the way toward light and hope.

A special mention goes to my dear friend, my soul confidant, Sanjay Shukla. Your empathetic ear and unwavering presence during our lengthy conversations were a balm to my troubled soul. Your kindness and care surpassed all bounds.

To my best friend, Ashutosh Matela, who selflessly chose to stand by me, relocating and offering unwavering support during a time of need. Your act of solidarity and friendship will forever be cherished.

I owe a debt of gratitude to the spiritual luminaries, psychologists, and psychiatrists whose profound writings offered insight and guidance. Their wisdom helped me navigate the intricate landscape of depression, fostering a holistic approach that empowered physical, mental, and spiritual rejuvenation.

This book stands as a testament to the collective wisdom, love, and support of these incredible individuals and communities, guiding others toward holistic healing and renewed well-being.

Yes, it is possible to heal your depression holistically such that you come out as a perennially stronger, peaceful and happy person.

With deepest appreciation,
Ashish Lal

NOTE FROM THE AUTHOR

As you delve into this ebook on healing depression via holistic methods, know that a video format of the course is also available. For those who find videos more engaging, consider exploring that option. The name of the full video course is "Beyond Stress and Depression" and is available on the RedAsh TV's website - www.redashtv.com. In fact, you can watch the first chapter for free now. However, if you prefer reading a book, fear not – it's right here for you.

A holistic approach towards healing depression is important. Whether you choose to read or watch, your journey to healing depression holistically begins now.

Stay fit!
Ashish Lal

CONTENTS

1 : UNDERSTANDING STRESS AND DEPRESSION

Hello everyone! I am Ashish Lal. Picture this: It's a very beautiful early morning at the beach, with the sea extending its warm welcome to you. Magic light hugs the entire city. It's so serene and peaceful. This is the right time and the right place to talk about how we can move from stress and go into a state of calm and peace.

These days you talk to a kid, a youth, a middle-aged person or even an old person, everybody seems to be so stressed out. The saddest part is that most of them believe that stress has to be an integral part of their practical lives. This is so untrue. Never ever believe that. You just need proper knowledge and application of that knowledge to be in a state of perennial peace and calm.

Research worldwide has shown that about 10% of men and about 20% of women suffer from a major depressive episode at some point in their lives.

This percentage might vary from country to country and culture to culture. Countries like China, India, U.S., Russia, Brazil, Indonesia, Nigeria, Pakistan, Bangladesh, Germany are some of the most depressed countries in the world. So, you can clearly see that economic prosperity or the lack of it is not the sole reason for depression. If I talk about my country, WHO has said that a whopping 36% of Indians are likely to suffer from a major depressive episode at some point in their lives. So, this is not a simple issue. It is a very serious issue and it must be addressed.

Depressed people are submerged in a sea of stressful thoughts. Such people suffer from one or more of these : excessive exhaustion, get angry easily, cry easily, cannot focus, cannot communicate clearly, are under confident, obsessively need to rush home after work, are preoccupied with gadgets, are continuously putting down colleagues on mails and social media or take a lot of time to sleep after going to bed.

Why am I talking about it? Am I a psychiatrist? No, I am not. But I have been through chronic depression for several years. I can empathize with people who've seen such low in their lives. And I can understand that. It's very painful.

When I was in that phase, almost always I used to have extremely stressful, insecure, fearful and negative thoughts. I rarely felt loved even a bit, always felt taken for granted. I used to be very sad from within, but on the outside, instead of crying, I used to get angry frequently. Confidence had become a thing of the past, though on the outside, I probably gave a very confident image. It used to take me 1.5 to 3.5 hours to sleep after going to bed. The very instant I used to wake up, I felt that strong tsunami of stress rush into the conscious mind. That showed that 24 / 7, even during sleep, I was extremely stressed from the subconscious. Only I know how broken and depressed I felt from within.

This was all while I was performing all my duties to the best of my abilities, doing my daily work, and everything that seemed normal to everybody else. But I know how painful it was.

However now, after a few years, my permanent state of being, most of the time, is of inner deep peace and happiness. It's not that I don't get stressed or sad or angry, but that happens very rarely. I used to take one and half hours to three and half hours to sleep; now it takes me almost 10 minutes only to sleep. In situations, especially negative situations, where I used to get very stressed out, now I can handle them very calmly. I'm mindful and aware of what I'm doing and I do what I need to do, and just move on.

Isn't it quite a transformation? If it is, shouldn't I share it with people across the globe and help them also achieve the same state? If you're one of those who is always happy, I wish and bless you with more happiness. If you're not, maybe this book will help.

"Heal Depression Holistically" is a book which covers psychological, physiological and spiritual methods to handle stress and depression.

We'll start with temporary solutions to deal with stress and go towards a destination where we find a state of permanent bliss. Yes, it is possible!

Even if you begin walking on this path, stress will gradually drop, organically. I have realized that this path is independent of any person or any situation. It is only dependent upon me.

Come, hold my hand. Let's Walk From Stress to Bliss. Will you?

2: THE MENTAL METHODS

In the 1st chapter, we came to a conclusion that we can go beyond stress and depression with the right knowledge and experience.

In this 2nd chapter, we'll talk about 4 steps that we can take to defeat depression in the initial stages itself. Different people can be depressed due to different reasons, but these methods will work for all. So, let's go!

The First Step Is To Share

Sharing is very powerful. It is so powerful that in the beginning of the depressive phase, it might be the only step you need to take to end that phase once and for all. However, do not over-share. Do not talk to anyone and everyone just because you feel good when you get an approval of your sad thoughts or just because somebody gives you an ear. It is not about quantity, it's about quality. Talk to those people who care about you and who are honest with you. We all have 2-3 such people in our lives. Don't we?

When I was in that phase, I used to talk to a few loved ones a few times. However, there were only two people with whom I could talk to almost on a daily basis for months at a stretch – my mother and my closest friend Sanjay. Though they were really caring and loved me a lot, they did not agree to whatever I said. They gave a very objective assessment of the situation which a person submerged in depression just cannot do.

It's a very good idea to talk to someone who has been through the same ordeal and has come out of it successfully. Don't talk to someone who has faced the same issue, but is still depressed. Such people will unconsciously push you into more darkness.

Suppose a loving father loses her 4 year old daughter to an accident, my suggestion of what he can do to move ahead in life would be so meaningless. However, if he meets another father whose child had died several years ago and who has come out stronger after a few years, his suggestions, even if they're the same, will make more sense to him as he can relate to him. You might think that your issue is unique but chances are high that millions must have been through it and successfully got over it. Go find that person. That person's suggestions would be priceless. People have come out of much graver and intense issues in life. Understand that whatever your issue is, it is not the end of the world. You'll find ways and people to help you go beyond it.

The Second Step Is To Get Busy

Most people would suggest that you need to get busy to distract yourself. But distracting is a very temporary solution. Distracting yourself is not the main motive. You need to get busy, but you need to get busy doing things that you love to do. We all have a job or something that we do most of the time in a day. But the time that we get apart from that, only do things that you love to do. That will help you sustain doing that for a very long time.

Like I love watching Hindi stand-up comedy and I used to give hours every single day to watch that. People thought I was having a ball of a time, but it was therapy for me. I also love writing. So in that depressive phase I completed writing a complete screenplay with dialogues of a full-length Hindi feature film. I also started writing my first book. Mind is very weird. It finds sadness addictive and intoxicating. So it wants you to just lie down, basically be sad, manipulate stories in your mind, in your favor. I had to literally push myself to open the laptop and start writing, whether it was good or bad, whether I wanted to do it or not. You just have to push yourself a few times before it becomes a habit; and doing things that you love heals you.

One very important aspect is to set goals. Set short term goals and long term goals. So the bottom-line is that with your work or what you do apart from your work that you love, set goals - long term goals and short term goals - that will motivate you. A deadline motivates you and helps you heal.

The Third Step Is To Break Your Patterns

As actors, we're regularly taught to break our patterns, even if it is only for sometime and even if we fall back to our old patterns very soon. That doesn't mean that if you have never had drugs, you go out and have a cocaine shot. No. Balance is important. There's no need to go to extremes to prove a point.

You must be having a typical way you do things the entire day. Suppose you wake up, check your mobile, take it to the washroom, there you brush your teeth with your right hand, then check your messages, do your morning chores, take your car and drive it on a certain path to your job, open your laptop at the office, work in a certain way, take breaks at definite time, leave for home at a fixed time, at home watch television, go on social media, chat with friends and then sleep.

Do you see the patterns? Then change them – wake up half an hour earlier, don't look at your mobile when you wake up, go to the washroom without your addictive mobile, brush your teeth not using your right hand but using your left hand, do your morning chores, take another route may be a longer one, work in a different way, take breaks at different times, leave half an hour later for home, do not watch television, or go on social media or chat with friends, instead may be just read a book, thank for good things of that day before sleeping and then go to sleep.

Do one or more of these and maybe after a few weeks, come back to your normal self. Then break some other pattern of yours. Every week or at least every month, you must be working on breaking one or more of your patterns. The freshness with which you live life will generate the happiness required to gradually kill depression.

The Fourth Step Is To Meet New People

Meet new people who don't know anything about your past, people who don't know that you are depressed. When you meet them don't talk about your depression initially. Meeting new people gives you a fresh perspective to life. It has been a major transformative method for me during depression. I met scores of people and among them I've made at least 25 very good friends with whom I can have long and meaningful conversations. They range from the age of 21 to the age of 35; they are of different states, different cultures, they speak different languages, they are different kinds of people. And that really helps. My method has been - when I meet them, I just listen. I don't talk too much, I just listen to them. I really care about what they are saying and then the friendship grows organically. If it doesn't grow then gracefully end it.

Try to meet people from different genders, different age groups, different countries, cultures, religion, cast, creed, color, people having different abilities, different likes and dislikes. It really helps. If you are uncomfortable talking to a stranger, you can also connect with people online and then meet face to face.

When you meet somebody, try to not have an agenda. Don't think that meeting them will help you get over your depression or bring something great in your life. Just sit with them. Just listen to what they are saying. Care about them. Spread love and you know what? Love heals! The more you give love, the more you get love!

Phases Of Depression

There are 3 phases of depression. The first phase is DENIAL, second is ACCEPTANCE and the third is MOVING ON.

The 4 steps we talked about helps you from the very first phase itself. It also helps you become a much more evolved person. Eventually it is the width and depth of our perception that determines the quality of our life. Isn't it?

3: THE PHYSICAL METHODS

In this chapter, we'll work on physiological aspects to deal with psychological stress.

We'll talk about 3 things:
1. **Exercise**
2. **Food**
3. **Sleep**

Exercise

Whenever you exercise, your body releases endorphins, a.k.a. "happy hormones", that make you feel happy. You must have heard of "runner's high", which is a "euphoric" feeling that a runner has after his run.

Do body weight exercises, swimming, outdoor sports, weight training, martial arts, Yoga, cycling, brisk walking, jogging, running, dancing or whichever form of physical exercise you love to do so that you can keep doing it for a long period of time.

Since 2009, I've been doing weight-training exercises with free weights and machines, mostly at the gym and sometimes at home. I've also been doing freehand exercises frequently at home or the gym. However, my true love is Yoga. Many don't know that Yoga comprises not just asanas i.e. different postures but also pranayamas, mudra, bandh and Dhyan (Dhyan means meditation).Since 2000, I've been regularly doing Yoga, primarily some of the Pranayamas, Asanas and Dhyan. They have a very powerful effect on our body, mind and soul.

Though all exercises have a powerful positive impact on curbing stress, there are some Pranayamas that are powerful beyond imagination in combating stress. Pranayamas directly impact your mind in an extremely positive way. Sometimes, in just a few weeks, it can cure mild or moderate depression that months of medication cannot do.

For all **Pranayamas**, sit in a comfortable posture with your back straight.

Your neck should also be straight and eyes closed. Even with eyes closed, your virtual line of vision should be parallel to the ground – not looking down or up. Have a gentle smile on your face. Never move any part of your body other than those you're working on – a Pranayama is an internal exercise, not an external one. Shaking or moving shoulders, neck, head is wrong – they should be absolutely still. Also, take rest in between when needed. Never do more than your comfort level, which will increase with time and practice.

Bhastrika Pranayama:

Take a deep breath in calmly, with both the nostrils, without exerting any force. After that with a little force, throw the air out with both the nose. Again inhale calmly and exhale with a little force.

You can do this at slow, medium and fast pace or a mix of all three. For example, you can do 20 times slow, 30 times medium and 50 times fast or you can do any one 100 times. All are beneficial.

Nadi Shodhan Pranayama:

With your right thumb, close your right nostril. Inhale very slowly from your left nostril. This is step 0. Step 0 is done just to begin the Pranayama and should not be repeated anytime again, except when taking a break and then again beginning.

Now do step 1. Close your left nostril using the middle and ring finger. Now exhale slowly and then inhale slowly from the same right nostril.

Now do step 2. Close your right nostril with your thumb and then exhale slowly first and then inhale slowly, both from the same left nostril.

Step 1 and 2 constitutes one round.

Nadi Shodhan Pranayama has 4 stages depending upon how long

you exhale, hold, inhale and hold. However, for beginners, let's keep it simple – keep the duration of exhalation and inhalation the same. Also, the breath should be so slow and smooth that if a small piece of cotton is kept below the nostrils, it should not shake at all because of inhalation or exhalation.

Bhramari Pranayama:

Close both your ears with your right and left index fingers.

Take a very slow and deep breath in. Then, while keeping your mouth shut, make a humming sound as long as you comfortably can. Now again take a very slow deep breath in, make a humming sound and so on and so forth.

In the end, lie down in **Shavasana**, the corpse pose, for about 5 to 10 minutes with a smile on your face and just witness the sensations created by these powerful Pranayamas in your body.

Witness from toe to head and back from head to toe. Repeat this till the sensations normalize. Note that from the 1st Pranayama, do not open your eyes even once till the time you're done with Shavasana when you need to sit down and open your eyes slowly. Pranayamas need to be done 3-4 hours after a heavy meal and 1-2 hours after a light meal.

If you want to do the exercises you love along with these Pranayamas, the entire physical activity session should end with these Pranayamas and not the other way around.

Food

It might take hours of lecture if we want to talk about what and how to eat, but we'll keep it short. Understand one thing – we're all natural beings. The more natural stuff we can eat, the better it is for our physical, mental and spiritual health. Try to avoid fast food, oily, sugary and packed items as much as possible. Try to eat home cooked food in minimal oil. Also, you should never feel hungry for more than 5 minutes or so. Eat either before you feel hungry or the moment you feel that hunger pang in your stomach. Tolerating hunger doesn't just make you weak and prone to several diseases, it also makes you gain more fat over time.

Many people start eating too many sugary items saying that they release endorphins and make you feel happy instantly. Yes, some of them do, but only for some time. Also, they cause a lot of harm. There are much healthier things to eat to release endorphins –

bananas, strawberries, oranges, nuts, grapes, sesame seeds etc.

More than what to eat or drink, it is important to discuss what not to eat or drink. Most people, when stressed, do too much smoking, drinking or drugs. You feel relaxed when you're in their effect, but after the effect is gone, the stress comes back manifolds. These things just mess with your intellect and because you cannot think those compulsive stressful thoughts in that state, you feel good for a while. I've never ever even tasted cigarettes, alcohol, drugs or for that matter any intoxicant whatsoever, but I've learnt to achieve a far more prolonged state of calm through age old permanent and powerful ways. We shall discuss them later. Let's try avoiding shortcuts that can short-circuit anytime; instead, let's try taking the right path even if it is longer. Longer and permanent is better than shorter and temporary.

Sleep

First things first – after a lot of research it has been found that an average human being needs to sleep everyday for a minimum of 7 hours and a maximum of 9 hours. Sleeping less than 6 hours or more than 10 hours have been found to create chronic and incurable lifestyle diseases. Depressed people either sleep very less or sleep a lot.

Secondly, sleeping for 8 hours from 4am to 12pm is not as effective as sleeping from 10 pm to 6 am. For those who cannot sleep early, I always say that at least "Sleep the very day you wake up!"

Most people who are depressed, stressed or anxious face this problem of not being able to sleep quickly. In the 1st chapter, I had mentioned that during my depressed phase, I used to take about 1.5 to 3.5 hours to sleep after going to bed, but now it takes only about 10 minutes. A form of meditation has helped me make such a drastic transformation. You can also follow it to gain its benefits.

When you go to bed, lie down in Shavasana on your back with hands on the sides and palms facing the sky. This is a meditation technique and not a Pranayama. In Pranayamas you alter how you breathe to have a positive impact. Here you do not alter the breath at all. You just witness the breath as it comes and goes. Your consciousness should flow with the breath – breath goes in, there's a pause, then it comes out and then there's a pause – count 1 in your mind. Then again the breath comes in, pause, goes out, pause – count 2. Focus should not be on counting which should be automatic. Focus should be on going in and out literally along with the breath. Don't just see the breath, flow along with it. Do not try to take deep breaths or shallow breaths, do not try to feel good or bad about the breath – as the breath comes in and goes out, just witness it without any reaction whatsoever to it. Suppose at the count of 18, your focus shifts to thoughts. When you realize it, do not try to stop them. Mind cannot focus on two things at the same time. So just bring your focus back on the breath and flow with it, and immediately the thoughts will drop on its own. Now start your count from 19. After a while, you won't even realize, your body and mind will get so relaxed that you'll fall into a deep sleep.

Practice this meditation till you fall asleep. Suppose you wake up at night and again have difficulty sleeping, practice this meditation again. Your body needs sleep because it needs 'rest'. This meditation has that 'resting' effect as well. Hence, even if your count goes till 300 or 500 or even more, before you fall asleep, it's not a waste of time – it's adding to your rest.

It is a very good idea to consult a psychologist or a psychiatrist. I have always been open to this idea. But primarily because of Pranayamas and Meditation, I could handle the situation myself.

I've never had to take a sleeping pill or any medicine prescribed to depressed patients. If you follow every suggestion given in this book, probably you'll also never need to have them.

4: THE SPIRITUAL METHODS

In this chapter, we'll go to the deepest level to rise above suffering and reach a state of constant bliss. No, the method is not physiological, not even psychological but spiritual. The moment I utter the word 'spiritual', most people equate it to being impractical. I'm here to tell you through my experience that spiritual understanding or just the beginning of it, will bring an immense amount of positive and practical transformations in your life that probably years of your so-called practical methods haven't been able to.

There's no religious connotation at all. A religious person can be spiritual but a spiritual person can be completely non-religious. What do I mean by the 'spiritual' path? Though there can be many answers, let me try to keep it simple. Anybody who understands that all our happiness or suffering are primarily dependent not on external situations or other people, but on what goes within us, and hence who works towards changing and evolving from within, is walking on the spiritual path.

Everything Within, Nothing Without

I'll use an example. Suppose somebody says or does something that makes you feel bad or happy. Where do you feel that feeling? Within yourself, right? Every single experience of your life that you've lived has been within you. Have you seen that the same depressing event that causes someone to commit suicide, causes some other person to grow into a much more stronger, successful and evolved person? It's all about how you handle things from within. So let's work on evolving ourselves from the inside, and not the outside.

The Control Experiment

Last year, I did something I call "The Control Experiment!" I enumerated the most important aspects, phases or decisions that shaped my entire life and brought me where I am today. I could come up with 32 of them.

S.No.	About	In Control	Comments
1	Birth	No	
2	Height	No	
3	Face	No	
4	Physique	Partially	If IIT mimicry hadn't happened, probably would have never thought of becoming an actor and hence never got this lean muscular physique
5	Family	No	
6	School	No	Parents decided for me
7	Going to Bokaro	Partially	If not known about IIT there, or if family did not stay there, would not have gone
8	Falling for someone	No	Nobody can control that
9	Being backstabbed the 1st time	No	Who backstabs can only control, not you
10	Being backstabbed the 2nd time	No	2nd time, it shows it's a habit of the other person
11	Being committed come what may	No	Taught by family - had I been born in not so idealistic family, would have ended relation soon
12	Arthritis	No	Happened because of random choice of exercise using a bullworker
13	Yoga	No	Because of wrong exercise, had this - at 18, I thought I'm doing it right
14	Continuing Yoga	Partially	If body would have been fine, I would have probably stopped after a point
15	IIT	Partially	3rd time got through only because of Yoga which was only because of Arthritis which happened because of random buying of bullworker
16	Corporate job	No	It was because of the society and family teaching me to do this - never imagined anything else could also be done
17	CAT	No	Gave my best but still could only reach 94 percentile & did not get an IIM call
18	Network business	Partially	If first job was great, probably I would have never thought of any other thing
19	Fights	Partially	Consistently bombarded by lying and cheating over years leads to subconscious anger & frustration, but could have ended relation; today no fights at all for years
20	Stamp on relationship	No	Because commitment was something that was because of the family I was born
21	Films	Partially	Theater stint, first job bad experience and not qualifying in the IIMs
22	Acting	No	Just happened as an IIT fresher; and then just hated my 1st job - had I loved, probably would have been doing a job today
23	Quitting job	Partially	Had I qualified in IIMs, I would have probably never quit job
24	1st movie WILD	No	Random meeting of Manav, ideation and then it just went on
25	Continuing WILD	Partially	Because it started, it had to be finished - because since childhood learnt that always take a job till the end, so this character made me do it more than anything else
26	Being backstabbed the 3rd time	No	3rd time it shows something seriously wrong in the basic deep character and attitude of the person, nobody can control except God's fruits to such repetitive bad karma
27	Took stamp off the relationship	No	Except for the extreme things happening, never ever would have done that come what may
28	RLi movie writing	Partially	Wrote during depression, that's why a little dark; depression wasn't in my control
29	Continuing in films	Yes	Even after everything bad happened, I did not quit - this was probably my decision but coming into films was not in my control
30	Teaching	No	Situations forced me into it, not at all in my control
31	NPOS movie writing and pre-production	Partially	Happened because someone told me of a book and an app - it just triggered this movie
32	Finding investors	Partially	If got good roles through auditions or had been born in a filmy family, might have got roles easily and never struggled to find an investor myself

Then I found that 19 of them were not in my control at all and happened because of my birth in a particular family, culture and country or because of the situation I was put into. 12 of them were partially in my control where I had to make a decision based on the situation that arose; however, the situations were unexpectedly thrown by life at me and in a way that was the only decision I could take.

Only 1 out of 32 I believe was a decision I could take irrespective of any situation or people around and that was to continue my unconditional struggle in films whatever be the result and even if it takes my entire life full of only failures.

| 29 | Continuing in films | Yes | Even after everything bad happened, I did not quit - this was probably my decision but coming into films was not in my control | 4 |

The results of this Control Experiment changed everything about my life, it just calmed me down, it almost put a brake to the continuous subconscious anxiety that we all have in trying to control people or things the way we want. My suggestion to you is do YOUR Control Experiment – it will help you let go of many things that you have been obsessively trying to control for a long long time.

Acceptance & Letting Go

Let's stop playing God by trying to control every situation and every person. Why? For the simple reason that WE CANNOT! So what to do? Let's learn to get into the acceptance mode. A very clichéd question that pops up is – "So should I accept defeat, lie lazy, not be ambitious, not try to push to get what I want?" Hold on, hold on. I don't mean that. Try to make the situation better where you can. The point is that where you know you cannot or should not change people or situation, learn to accept wholeheartedly. For example, if someone towards whom you've been loyal is cheating on you, you should accept this fact instead of living in denial. Then talk it out with your partner to assess if the person really feels sorry or is it just drama because she has been caught red handed. Suppose the latter case holds good, and end the relationship once and for all. And then accept that the relationship has ended and don't try to bring her back even when you feel really weak. That is the true meaning of acceptance. The bottom-line is to leave the subconscious anxiety by accepting wholeheartedly whatever happened in the past and be ready to accept with open arms whatever out of your control things will happen in the future.

Thoughts

I always say this – "The greatest addiction of the human race is not drinking, it's 24x7 thinking!" Are thoughts bad? Yes and no. If thoughts are to plan for the future or take lessons from the past or to help you do whatever you're doing at this moment, then they are great. However, if thoughts are obsessive stressful thoughts about your past, anxious fearful thoughts about your future, or random thoughts, positive or negative, that have been coming in a loop for a long, long time, then it's sickness. Thoughts are given undue importance. We actually believe that we cannot and in fact should not stop our thinking. We also believe that we 'always' think - no, we don't. Also, we think that for a blissful life, the goal is to replace negative thoughts with positive thoughts – no, the goal is to replace thoughts with no thoughts, till they're really needed. Shocked? Don't be.

DO YOU KNOW THAT MOST OF THE TIMES, YOU DO NOT THINK OF THE NEXT SENTENCE YOU SPEAK? Where does that come from? It is a myth that your life is functional only because of your thoughts.

DO YOU KNOW THAT THE GREATEST CREATIVE IDEAS AND THE MOST BLISSFUL EXPERIENCES COME IN A STATE OF THOUGHTLESSNESS?

DO YOU KNOW THAT IT IS POSSIBLE, WITH CONSISTENT EFFORT, TO HAVE NO THOUGHTS AT ALL TILL THE TIME YOU REALLY NEED TO THINK? When you do need them, thoughts will be more effective.

DO YOU KNOW THAT MOST OF THE TIMES, TO GET THE BEST RESULTS IN PRACTICAL LIFE, WE JUST DO NOT NEED TO THINK AT ALL? Then what do we need to do? We need to just be in the NOW and be completely attentive to the good or the bad that we're doing or that is happening right now.

DO YOU KNOW THAT MOST OF THE TIMES, YOUR MENTAL STRESS IS ONLY AND ONLY AND ONLY BECAUSE OF THE THOUGHTS OF THE PAST OR THE FUTURE? There is rarely any stress in the present moment, in the NOW.

So in one line, to move from stress to bliss, you need to be completely engrossed in the NOW. Life is from now to now to now, it is a series of NOWs. All that you have is the NOW. All that you can do is only in the NOW. Even if you want to do something next Friday, you can only do it when that Friday's NOW comes. So the entire point boils down to – how can you learn to live in the now so that you don't have unnecessary thoughts? For that it is said that when you don't have thoughts, then you live in the NOW. It's very tricky. Do you think so? No, it is not. Let us learn how to achieve this state of thoughtlessness and living in the now.

It is very helpful to read books written by enlightened spiritual masters over the centuries. What is important is to read every single day, even if it is only for 10 minutes. Every day you need to feed yourself with some priceless wisdom. In these books, you'll find that almost every enlightened master confirms that meditation is probably the most powerful means to realize who we truly are, to realize the ultimate unconditional bliss that is always there within us. True meditation means to reach the state of complete thoughtlessness clubbed with complete awareness. You can achieve thoughtlessness in sleep as well, but it is devoid of awareness – and that's what creates all the difference. In India and some other parts of the world, for thousands of years, spiritual masters have been using different techniques of meditation. I'll try to teach you one of them in the next chapter "Guided Meditation". Without doing over-analysis of your childhood or past, just 20-60 minutes of daily practice of this meditation can directly and indirectly cure you of stress from the deepest level. There's no limit to how much you can increase the duration or frequency of this practice – the more, the better!

5: GUIDED MEDITATION

Sit down in a comfortable posture, with your back straight and your neck also straight. Close your eyes. The vision of your eyes should be parallel to the ground. Don't look down, don't look up. Even when your eyes are closed there is a vision line. So the entire backbone with the neck is straight.

During the day, do you ever put an effort to breathe? No, you don't. Similarly here we will not put any effort to breathe. We'll just observe the breath. So the breath comes in, pauses. Goes out, pauses. Comes in, pauses. Goes out, pauses. We will focus on the breath. And we will not only focus on the breath, we will also bring our consciousness to the breath and move along with it.

We will add one more thing. Once it goes in, pause. Once it goes out, pause. We count 1. Again, you go with the breath. In, pause. Out, pause. Count 2. Now the focus should not be on the counting. It should happen naturally.

The focus should be on the breath. And you have to travel along with the breath. Your reaction should be neutral. Don't be attached to the breath. Don't think this breath is good, this breath is bad. Just see, as a witness. As a third person. Just see as it is. Without any positive or negative image attached to that breath.

If you are breathing shallow, let it be shallow. If you are breathing deep, let it be deep. Suppose at the count of 18 your mind suddenly starts wondering and you don't even realise that you are thinking and not meditating. The moment you realise that you are not meditating but thinking, don't try to stop your thoughts. Nothing forceful has to be done in meditation. Everything should be organic. The mind has a property. It cannot focus on two things at the same time. So if you are having thoughts that means your focus is on the thoughts. To let the thoughts drop on its own you just need to bring back your focus on the breath. The moment the focus comes back on the breath, thoughts just drop organically. Then you start counting from 18. Many practitioners count from 1. But I would suggest you start the count from 18. If you don't remember from where you started thinking, then whatever number you remember last counted say 12, start from there. Keep on. This can be endless. This can be 100, 200,300, 500, 1000, 10,000, anything. The longer you meditate the better you feel.

This meditation will gradually help you remove the mud, the mist of obsessive thoughts from your mind. When your mind becomes still, you can now see things more as they are instead of giving it exaggerated meanings. You'll be able to accept situations and people more than ever before. Your entire perspective towards life will be a much more evolved one. And hence your life will be much more evolved, happy and blissful. Every step on this path helps us get closer to the eternal bliss that is within us. Don't be disheartened if sometimes your mind behaves in your old ways. Come back to the right path again and keep walking.

Meditation should not be a chore. It should be a way of life. Slow down in your life. Why so much hurry? What do you fear losing? Anything that is real is not lost; anything that is lost is not real. Too philosophical? Ok, let's talk about what to do practically and that is to be completely focused in the NOW.

IF YOU'RE EATING JUST EAT,
IF YOU'RE WIPING YOUR HANDS JUST WIPE YOUR HANDS,
IF YOU'RE GIVING A PRESENTATION JUST GIVE YOUR PRESENTATION,
IF YOU'RE TALKING JUST TALK, IF YOU'RE LISTENING JUST LISTEN,
IF YOU'RE ACTING JUST ACT, IF YOU'RE WATCHING JUST WATCH –
JUST BE, DON'T THINK ALL THE TIME. THINK ONLY WHEN IT IS ABSOLUTELY NEEDED.

In this meditation, if you notice, what you're doing is being in the now because the breath is never in the past or the future but always and only in the now. Whenever during the day, you have unnecessary thoughts, pulling you into the past or pushing you into the future, be aware of them and without trying to stop them, just bring your focus back on the work you're doing and the thoughts will drop on its own.

Another method to get out of the useless thought loop is to focus on your breath for a count of 5-10 only which will help you bring back your full attention to your work. Another strange method that works for me is to force my lips to smile and God knows how, thoughts just drop and I come back in the now. Remember, to go from stress to bliss, live in the now every moment and using meditation, try to touch your true nature within, which is of ultimate bliss, forever and ever.

CONCLUSION

I've walked a few steps on this spiritual path and found an enormous unbelievable and almost miraculous change in the quality of my life from within. Millions of people from over thousands of years have achieved a much higher state of bliss walking on the same path.

Psychological and physiological methods work at a certain level of the root, but the spiritual method works at the bottommost part of the root. It might sound strange to many, but walking on this spiritual path has also helped me in my professional life by leaps and bounds.

A calm and a clear mind always produces more creative and effective results. Walking on this combination of psychological, physiological and spiritual path, will take you towards the life of bliss you want to have from within.

I'm on this holistic path every single day - it's a lifestyle now. Come hold my hand, let's walk from stress to bliss! Will you?

ABOUT THE AUTHOR

Ashish Lal

By education, Ashish Lal is a B.Tech. in Civil Engineering from one of the world's most respected universities - IIT (Indian Institute of Technology), Delhi. After working in a multinational firm for a few years in the Data Analytics domain, Ashish left the corporate world to pursue his dream of making a career in the Hindi film industry, popularly known as Bollywood. He is a reputed actor, writer and filmmaker. He also owns his 15-year-old Mumbai-based film production house RedAsh Films Pvt. Ltd. As an actor, in the last decade, Ashish has done lead roles in several film, TV and web projects with many veterans and popular Indian actors.

Ashish firmly believes in holistic wellbeing. He battled depression for 3 years but came out permanently stronger using physical, mental and spiritual methods in such a way that even extremely stressful and devastating situations can't take his inherent peace and happiness away. The wisdom he gained during that phase was priceless - only someone who has gone through such a phase and came out wiser can teach others how to practically do it. He has created a detailed course on attaining holistic mental health. It is available in both video as "Beyond Stress & Depression" and ebook format as "Heal Depression Holistically".

Since 2000, Ashish has been consistently doing Yoga - asanas, pranayamas, and meditation. Since 2009, Ashish has practised scientific nutrition and also been regularly doing Gym weight training and Freehand bodyweight exercises.

Apart from this, Ashish also dedicated more than 3.5 years to researching, writing and creating another exhaustive course on physical health - "Lifelong Scientific Fitness - the Encyclopedia of Nutrition Science, Gym Training (130+ exercises), Freehand Exercises (55+ exercises) & Yoga (20+ exercises)". It is available as a video course and also as a 7-part ebook series.

Moreover, Ashish has created a detailed course on healing asthma using 3-time tested alternative therapies "Heal Asthma using Yoga Ayurveda & Nutritional Therapy. It is also available in both video and ebook format.

Ashish remains super-fit physically, mentally and spiritually - not temporarily, but 365 days a year, year after year, by following natural and scientific time-tested methods for holistic fitness. To help others, he shares his wisdom and experience through exhaustive and holistic books and video courses on physical fitness, mental health & asthma. His fitness mantra is - "Stay permanently fit, scientifically & holistically!"

BOOKS BY THIS AUTHOR

Heal Asthma Via Alternative Therapies

Heal Depression Holistically

Forever Fit Scientifically: Part 1 - Fundamentals

Forever Fit Scientifically: Part 2 - Nutrition

Forever Fit Scientifically: Part 3 - Gym

Forever Fit Scientifically: Part 4 - Freehand Exercises

Forever Fit Scientifically: Part 5 - Yoga

Forever Fit Scientifically: Part 6 - Become Your Own Trainer And Nutritionist

Forever Fit Scientifically: Part 7 - Be The Change